I0182876

A work in progress
This is the sixth edition - February 2016
In the Mirror,
Bible language becomes heart to heart
whispers of grace!

Mirror Word Logo by: Wilna Furstenburg

Cover Design by: Bryce Phelps and Sean Osmond

Published by Mirror Word Publishing

The Mirror Bible is also available as an iPhone or Android mobile app on the following website, www.mirrorbible.com

Should you wish to order printed copies in bulk, [10 or more] pls contact us at info@mirrorword.net

Contact us if you wish to help sponsor Mirror Bibles in Spanish, Shona or Xhosa.

 Highly recommended books by the same author: Divine Embrace, God Believes in You, Done!,

Children's book, The Eagle Story, by Lydia and Francois du Toit, beautifully illustrated by Carla Krige

The Mirror Bible, Divine Embrace God Believes in You and The Logic of His Love are also abailable on Kindle

Francois' ministry page is www.mirrorword.net

Subscribe to Francois facebook updates http://www.facebook.com/francois.toit

The Mirror Translation fb group http://www.facebook.com/groups/179109018883718/
ISBN 978-0-9921769-4-5

MirrorWORD

THE MIRROR

The Mirror is a paraphrased translation from the Greek text. While strictly following the literal meaning of the original, sentences have been constructed so that the larger meaning is continually emphasized by means of an expanded text.

Some clarifying notes are included in italics. This is a paraphrased study rather than a literal translation. While the detailed shades of meaning of every Greek word have been closely studied, this is done taking into account the consistent context of the entire chapter within the wider epistle, and bearing in mind the full context of Jesus and his finished work, which is what the message of the Bible is all about

To assist the reader in their study, I have numerically superscripted the Greek word and corresponded it with the closest English word in the italicized commentary that follows. This is to create a direct comparison of words between the two languages.

I translated several Pauline epistles 25 years ago called the Ruach Translation. In 2006 I started with the Mirror Translation. This is an ongoing process and will eventually include the entire New Testament as well as select portions of the Old Testament.

Completed books as of February 2016 are:
John's Gospel, Romans, 1 Corinthians, 2 Corinthians,
Galatians, Ephesians, Philippians, Colossians,
1 Thessalonians, 2 Timothy, Titus, Hebrews, James, 1
John, In Progress: 1 Peter 1,2; 2 Peter 1.

INTRODUCTION TO PHILIPPIANS

Paul, Silas, Timothy and Luke visited Philippe and founded the first church in Europe on Paul's second missionary journey around A.D. 50 (Acts 16:11-40)

This letter was written in about 61 A.D. from Rome while Paul was under house arrest.

He writes from a place of strength and joy to encourage his dear friends in Philippi, who were also facing many contradictions.

Phil 1:20 My immediate circumstances do not distract from my message! I am convinced that our conversation now and always will continue to give accurate account of the magnificence of Christ. The message is incarnate in me; whether I live or die, it makes no difference.

Phil 1:21 Christ defines my life; death cannot threaten or diminish that.

Phil 2:12 "Not only in my presence but much more in my absence..." Paul knew that he would be more present in his message than in his person! Ministry success is not measured by how many partners you can congregate, but how absent you can preach yourself!

Phil 3:1 The conclusion of your faith is extreme gladness in the Lord. He is your constant reference to bliss! I am not just saying this to be repetitive; joy is your fortress! There is no safer place to be, but to be ecstatically happy!

Paul encourages them not to allow religion to distract from the delight of romance.

Phil 3:7 The sum total of my religious pedigree and sincere devotion amounts to zero! What we have been gifted with in Christ has reduced what once seemed so important, to meaningless information. To esteem the law is to your loss! Faith is your profit.

Phil 3:8 In fact, I have come to the conclusion that every association I have had with that which defined me before as a devout Jew, is by far eclipsed by what I have gained in knowing the Messiah. Jesus Christ and his masterful redemption define me now. Religion is like dog pooh; and it stinks, avoid stepping in it!

Phil 4:4 Joy is not a luxury option; joy is your constant! Your union in the Lord is your permanent source of delight; so I might as well say it again, rejoice in the Lord always!

Phil 4:6 Let no anxiety about anything ¹distract you!

Phil 4:11 I have discovered my "I am-ness" and found that I am fully ¹self sufficient, whatever the circumstance. *(Self sufficient, ¹**autarkes**, self complacent, the feeling you have when you are completely satisfied with yourself.)*

Phil 4:13 In every situation I am strong in the one who empowers me from within to be who I am! *(Paul lived his life in touch with this place within himself. He discovered that the same I am-ness that Jesus walked in, was mirrored in him! I am what I am by the grace of God! 1 Cor 15:10)*

PHILIPPIANS Chaper 1

1:1 Paul and Timothy address all the saints in Christ Jesus in Philippi, including your leadership team, both the [1]overseers and the [2]deacons. *(Overseer, [1]episkopos, from epi, indicating continues influence upon, and skopos, "scope" to see the overall picture, [2]diakonos, from diako, to run errands, to pursue; see Phil 3:14.)*

1:2 The Father's favor joins our lives inseparably in the Lordship of Jesus Christ.

1:3 The thought of you always inspires me with joy and gratitude to God.

1:4 Praying for you is certainly not a job it is more like poetry; I joyfully anticipate the outcome of my prayers for you!

1:5 Our blissful participation in everything that the gospel communicates does not age. The freshness of our first encounter continues to this very day.

1:6 I possess an inward certainty about you, confident that he who is the [1]initiator of the good work within you is also the one who executes its completeness as mirrored in Jesus Christ, who is the light of day. He is the fullness of time. *(Initiator, [1]enarche, to rehearse from the beginning. See Eccl 3:15, "that which has been is now; and that which is to be has already been!")*

1:7 I am not being presumptuous to be this persuaded about you. In the context of our redeemed innocence I cannot think of you any differently; I have you in my heart! Your committed friendship in my imprisonment is of great encouragement to me in our combined defense and confirmation of the gospel. We are in this together! We are joint participants in the same grace. My grace is your grace.

1:8 God knows my intense longing for you! It is with the tender affections of Jesus Christ!

1:9 It is my desire for each one of you, that the realization of ¹love's completeness in you will increasingly burst through all boundaries, and that every sphere of your relationship with others will be greatly impacted by your intimate acquaintance with love. *(The word ¹agape is a compound word from ago, which means to lead as a shepherd leads his sheep, and pao, which means rest! His love leads me into his rest; into the full realization of his finished work! Agape is Psalm 23 in one word. "By the waters of reflection my soul remembers who I am.")*

1:10 I urge you to examine this agape-love with the utmost scrutiny, just like when a diamond is viewed in the full sunlight to prove its flawless perfection. I dare you to take love to its ultimate conclusion! There is no offence in love, as evidenced in Jesus Christ who is the light of day. *(If the diamond is flawless to begin with, every possible test will prove its perfection; how someone might respond to love's initiative is not the point, love's ultimate test was concluded on the cross. Truth does not become true by popular vote; someone's ignorance or indifference cannot change the truth.)*

1:11 You have been fully furnished with the harvest of your redeemed innocence and righteousness which Jesus Christ labored for! This is what the glorious intent of God is all about! Celebrate him!

1:12 I wish to encourage you dear friends that the opposition that I face, which was meant to defeat the gospel has only served to advance it!

1:13 The prison has become my pulpit! All the soldiers in the Governor's guard and everyone involved in the palace have learnt about my message. They know that I am not their prisoner but that I am enclosed in Christ.

1:14 My imprisonment has also persuaded many believers in the Lord to speak the word with fearless courage.

1:15 Some slander the message and others speak with passion and delightful certainty.

1:16 There are those who wish to get mileage out of my predicament for their own agenda.

1:17 Others again are completely love inspired and in full support with me in my defense of the gospel!

1:18 I am thrilled! Christ is the topic of conversation everywhere! Even the negative publicity continues to advertise him!

1:19 I can just see how the Spirit of Jesus Christ, like a [1]conductor of music takes all of this together with your prayers and turn it into a concert that celebrates salvation! *(The word, [1]epichoregeo, comes from epi, a preposition of position, over, in charge, + chorus,* *choir, orchestra, or dance + **ago**, meaning to lead as a shepherd leads his sheep; thus, the leader of a dance or the conductor of music.)*

1:20 My ¹thoughts are not trapped in my head! They roam free in expectation that I will not be ashamed by any contradiction! My ²immediate circumstances do not distract from my message! I am convinced that our ²conversation now and always will continue to give accurate account of the magnificence of Christ. The message is incarnate in me; whether I live or die, it makes no difference. *(The word, ¹**apo-karadokia** is a compound word with 3 parts, **apo**, away from, **kara**, head and **dokeo**, thought. The word ²**parrhesia**, from **para**, a preposition indicating close proximity, a thing proceeding from a sphere of influence, with a suggestion of union of place of residence, to have sprung from its author and giver, originating from, denoting the point from which an action originates, intimate connection; and **rhesia**, conversation.)*

1:21 Christ defines my life; death cannot threaten or diminish that.

1:22 To be alive now is to feast on the harvest of your faith! I cannot tell when I shall lift up the anchor of the flesh and sail away! It doesn't really matter to me. *(The word, ¹**aihreomai**, from **airo**, to lift the anchor and sail away.)*

1:23 I am often torn between these two thoughts. I have this strong yearning to step out of the confines of this body into the immediate embrace of Christ!

Can you imagine the awesomeness of that!

1:24 Yet this gospel has my [1]arm twisted and locked behind my back; I am therefore determined to remain in the body for your sakes. *(The word, [1]anagke, suggests to have the arm twisted and locked behind one's back. See 1 Cor 9:16.)*

1:25 I am certain that my time with you will inspire the happy progress of your pioneering faith!

1:26 The joy of our union in Christ knows no limits! We have so much reason to celebrate! I can just imagine the eruptions of bliss should I be there with you right now in person!

1:27 The [1]one essential thing that would fully engage the focus of your earthly citizenship is the fact that your daily conduct communicates [2]like value and gives context to the gospel of Christ! So whether I am present with you to witness your steadfastness with my own eyes, or absent, our spiritual [3]union and single mindedness will be equally evident. *(The word [1]monon, points to that which is singled out as most essential; the word [2]axios, means, having the weight of another thing of like value, worth as much. Psyche, Greek, pshuche, suggests consciousness, mental attitude, awareness. Paul desires to express an inseparable togetherness; [3]sunathleo, athletic contest. Bicycle racing uses the term peloton; where the riders are strongest and fastest when they ride in the so-called "peloton", which is a densely packed group of riders, sheltering in each others' draft. In a mass-start race, most of the competitors usually end up in one large peloton for most of the race. The word is French, from a term that means rolled up in a ball.)*

1:28 Your brave fearlessness in the face of every kind of obstacle is a sure sign to those who oppose you that their efforts are futile. Your triumphant attitude makes salvation even more apparent. *(There is no counterfeit; God has no competition! Religion's self-help programs of salvation do not threaten him!)*

1:29 Because of the grace that you are gifted with in Christ, whatever you might suffer on behalf of him can never distract from what faith knows to be true about you!

1:30 Our faith is on exhibit in the same public ¹arena; we are not spectators of one another's endurance, but co-witnesses thereof. We mirror one another triumphantly. *(The word, ¹agon, refers to the place of contest, the arena or stadium.)*

PHILIPPIANS Chaper 2

2:1 In Christ our [1]association is most intimate; we [2]articulate his love story; entwined in spirit communion and tender affections. *(The word [1]parakaleo, from **para**, a preposition indicating close proximity, a thing proceeding from a sphere of influence, with a suggestion of union of place of residence, to sprung from its author and giver, originating from, denoting the point from which an action originates, intimate connection, and **kaleo**, to identify by name, to surname. The word [2]**paramuthion**, is from **para** + **muthos**, a myth or tale, a story of instruction, told in heart to heart language.)*

2:2 Your Christ mindedness completes my delight! You co-echo the same agape; we are soul mates, resonating the same thoughts.

2:3 No hidden agenda with a compromised mixture of leaven or empty philosophical flattery can match a mind that genuinely values others above oneself

2:4 To discover your own completeness in Christ frees you to turn your attention away from yourself to others!

2:5 The way Jesus saw himself is the only valid way to see yourself!

2:6 His being God's equal in form and likeness was official; his sonship did not steal the limelight from his Father! Neither did his humanity distract from the deity of God!

2:7 His mission however, was not to prove his deity but to embrace our humanity. Emptied of his reputation as God, he fully embraced our physical human form; born in our resemblance he identified himself as the servant of the human race. His love enslaved him to us!

2:8 And so we have the drama of the cross in context: the man Jesus Christ who is fully God, becomes fully man to the extent of willingly dying humanity's death at the hands of his own creation. He embraced the curse and shame of the lowest kind in dying a criminal's death.

2:9 From this place of utter humiliation, God exalted him to the highest rank. God graced Jesus with a Name that is far [1]above as well as equally representative of every other name; *(The word, [1]uper, means above, also instead, or for the sake of). The name of Jesus endorses his mission as fully accomplished! He is the Savior of the world! Titus 2:11 The grace of God shines as bright as day making the salvation of humankind undeniably visible. [Clarence Jordan translates this, "For God's undeserved kindness has burst in upon us, bringing a new lease on life for all mankind."] See also Eph 3:15, Every family in heaven and on earth originates in him; his is mankind's family name and he remains the authentic identity of every nation.)*

2:10 What his name unveils will persuade every creature of their redemption! Every knee in heaven and upon the earth and under the earth shall bow in spontaneous worship!

2:11 Also every tongue will voice and resonate the

PHILIPPIANS Chaper 2

same devotion to his unquestionable Lordship as the Redeemer of life! Jesus Christ has glorified God as the Father of creation! This is the ultimate conclusion of the Father's ¹intent! *(The word ¹doxa, intent, opinion, often translated, glory. Rev 5:13 And I heard every creature in heaven and on earth and under the earth and in the sea, and all therein, saying, "To him who sits upon the throne and to the Lamb be blessing and honor and glory and might for ever and ever!")*

2:12 Considering this amazing outcome of what our faith sees and celebrates I strongly urge you my darling friends to continue to have your ¹ears tuned to that which inspires your conduct to give full expression to the detail of your own salvation in a most personal and practical way. See salvation in its earth shattering awesome and ultimate conclusion. I know that my personal presence encourages you greatly but now I want you to realize an inspiration in my absence that supersedes anything you've known before. This would mean that even if you were never to see my face again or receive another Epistle from me, it will make no difference at all to your faith! *(The success of Paul's ministry was not to enslave people to him but to his gospel! He knew that he would be more present in his message than in his person! Ministry success is not measured by how many partners you can congregate, but by how absent you can preach yourself! The word often translated, obedience, is the word ¹upoakoo, to be under the inspired influence of what you hear.)*

PHILIPPIANS Chapter 2

2:13 Discover God himself as your inexhaustible inner source; he ignites you with both the desire and energy that matches his own delight!

2:14 Your entire life is a poem; any undercurrent murmuring or argumentative debating would be completely out of place! Do not let such issues disrupt the rhythm of your conversation.

2:15 Your flawless innocence radiates attraction as beacons of light in the midst of a people who have forgotten their true sonship and whose lives have become distorted and perverse. *(In this verse Paul quotes Deut 32:5 from the Greek Septuagint translation of the Hebrew text, with reference to Deut 32:4,5 &18. In context God's perfect workmanship as Father of mankind is forgotten; people have become "crooked and perverse" twisted and distorted out of their true pattern of sonship. Deut 32:18 says, you have forgotten the Rock that begot you and have gotten out of step with the God who [1]danced with you! Hebrew, [1]khul or kheel.)*

2:16 Your lives [1]echo-exhibit the [2]logic of the message of life. You are positioned like the stars in the night sky, superimposed and radiating light, which shining pierces the darkness. Thus you [3]confirm the day of the Lord and [3]complete my joy! You are my wreath of honor and [3]proof that I did not run my race in vain. *(The word, [1]epecho, is from epi, to superimpose, and echo, to hold, echo resonance. The word of life, [2]logos, it embodies a conception or idea, thought, logic. The preposition [3]eis, suggests a point reached in conclusion. See Col 1:29 Your completeness in Christ is not a remote goal, but your immediate reference! My labor now* *exceeds any zeal that I previously knew under the duty-driven law of willpower. I am laboring beyond the point of exhaustion, striving with intense resolve with all the energy that he mightily inspires within me.)*

2:17 I want you to see my ministry to you as wine poured out upon the altar of your faith. I rejoice in the thought that we drink from the same source and therefore celebrate a mutual joy!

2:18 Whatever you may suffer only concludes in joy! *(Joy is a bold declaraticn, in the face of severe danger and suffering, that contradiction does not define us or have the final say in our lives. We know that whether we live or die, our message is unstoppable and that it is conquering the world.)*

2:19 I trust the Lord that I will be able to send Timothy to you soon; this will be to me as if I am there personally with you!

2:20 I have no one here that share my heart more fully; I know that he will take care of you with utmost concern.

2:21 Sadly there are many in ministry with a selfish agenda

2:22 I do not need to tell you anything about Timothy because you already know his worth! We have labored together in the gospel in the closest possible association; we are like father and son in joint partnership.

2:23 I would like to send him to you immediately,

but I am just waiting to see how things here turn out for me.

2:24 I obviously would be very keen to join him shortly! I trust in the Lord for a positive outcome in my trial.

2:25 I feel urgent about sending Epaphrodites to you immediately; he is my brother, fellow worker and co-campaigner. You initially sent him to help me and now I am returning the favor!

2:26 He longs for you and really misses you. He felt quite distressed when he heard of your concern for him when he was so sick.

2:27 He nearly died but thank God for his mercy, not just for Epaphroditus' sake but for ours also! I cannot imagine the grief we would have suffered had we lost him!

2:28 I am sending him to you without delay; knowing what joy he will be to you is already such a comfort to me!

2:29 The immense value of his life is to be celebrated with a massive bliss-party when he arrives! Oh the joy to love one another in the Lord!

2:30 I so honor his total commitment to the work of Christ; he had no problem to risk his life to serve me on your behalf!

3:1 The conclusion of your faith is extreme gladness in the Lord. He is your constant reference to bliss! I am not just saying this to be repetitive; joy is your fortress! There is no safer place to be, but to be ecstatically happy!

3:2 The circumcision party are the enemies of your faith and freedom! They work with an evil agenda! Be on your guard for them just like you would avoid a vicious hound on the loose! They have their knives in for you!

3:3 We give "circumcision" its true spiritual meaning! Our worship is not defined by anything external that would even remotely resemble the law of works and religious rituals! We worship God in the certainty of our redeemed innocence and rejoice in the finished work of Jesus Christ. Faith-righteousness gives substance to spiritual worship; the flesh occupies the religious mind with its own futile efforts to attain to righteousness. I am convinced that circumcision or any work of the law can add nothing to the righteousness that Jesus secured on our behalf.

3:4 I have more reason than anyone else to rely on my years of diligent and most sincere devotion to Jewish sentiment and rituals. If gaining God's approval had anything to do with striving and personal effort I would beat the best in the business! My pedigree is obvious:

3:5 I received the famous cut when I was 8 days

old, exactly as the law prescribed. I am Israeli by birth; the head of my tribe is Benjamin. I am a Hebrew of the Hebrews! In my observance of the law I belonged to the strictest party; I was proud to be a Pharisee. *(Rachel was the darling wife of Jacob; she died while giving birth to Benjamin; also the two tribes that did not revolt were Benjamin and Judah. By saying that he is a Hebrew of the Hebrews Paul emphasises that his lineage from both parents side was not mixed with any Gentile blood.)*

3:6 The extremities of my fervor was demonstrated in the way I fiercely opposed and persecuted anyone who identified themselves in Christ. *(The so-called ekklesia.)* If keeping the law and these credentials could possibly have given me a blameless standing before God, I had it made!

3:7 The sum total of my religious pedigree and sincere devotion amounts to zero! What we have been gifted with in Christ has reduced what once seemed so important, to meaningless information. To esteem the law is to your loss! Faith is your profit.

3:8 In fact, I have come to the conclusion that every association I have had with that which defined me before as a devout Jew, is by far eclipsed by what I have gained in knowing the Messiah. Jesus Christ and his masterful redemption define me now. Religion is like dog pooh; and it stinks, avoid stepping in it!

3:9 So here I am; found in Christ! I was looking in

the wrong place all along! My own duty- and guilt-driven religious endeavor snared me in the cul-de-sac maize of self-righteousness, sponsored by the law of works! The faith of Christ reveals my identity; righteousness defines who God believes that I really am. This righteousness is sourced in God and endorses the authority of faith. *(Faith is a fairy tale if Jesus is not the substance of it!)*

3:10 Oh to comprehend the dynamic of his resurrection! His resurrection is evidence of our righteousness! In the revelation of God's economy of inclusion, I actually co-suffered with him and co-died together with Christ! *(Because I was already fully represented in his sufferings, his death and resurrection, I am greatly inspired when faced with contradictions now!)*

3:11 When confronted with death, I actually come [1]face to face with my own resurrection! *(The word [1]katantao, from kata + anti, to come to a place over against, opposite another, face to face. 1 Cor 15:18 No resurrection implies no hope for anyone beyond the grave; it makes no difference whether you believed that you were included in Christ's death or not. 1 Cor 15:19 If our hope in Christ was restricted to only benefit us in this life then imagine the severity of our disappointment if it all had to come to an abrupt end when we died. 1 Cor 15:20 However this very moment the risen Christ represents everyone who has ever died; exactly like how the first fruit would represent the complete harvest. 1 Cor 15:21 The same humanity who died in a man was raised again in a man. 1 Cor 15:22 In Adam all died; in Christ all are made alive.)*

3:12 There may be blurry edges to my ¹comprehending the full scope of resurrection life beyond
the grave; but I pursue the complete conclusion of
co-comprehending and ²fully grasping exactly that
which Jesus Christ knew all along about me when
he died my death; and to see me in his faith where
I am so perfectly included when he rescued and
raised me out of the grasp of death! *(The word, ¹lambano, means to comprehend, to grasp, to identify with. 1
Cor 13:12 To know even as I have always been known! The
word ²katalambano, from kata, which here strengthens
the verb lambano, thus to entirely grasp; to come to terms
with, to make one's own. The KJV reads, "that I may apprehend that for which also I am apprehended of by Christ
Jesus.")*

3:13 I am not boasting about this new found righteousness as if I came up with the idea; on the contrary, I have distanced myself from everything the
DIY-system of the law of works and willpower previously represented in my reference; now I am fully
engaged with that which the prophetic pointed to.
Christ is what we were reaching for all along! Here
he is ¹in our face; within our immediate grasp! *(The
DIY-system, is the fruit of the 'do it yourself-tree'. The
word ¹emprosthen, from en, in, and pros, that which is
right in front of me!)*

3:14 I have the prize of mankind's redeemed innocence in full view; just like a champion athlete in
the public games I refuse to be distracted by anything else. God has ¹invited us in Christ, to lift up

our eyes and realize our identity in him. *(The word, [1]klesis, invitation, from kaleo, to surname, to identify by name. While the law engages one with that which is below, faith captivates our gaze to only see that which is above, where we are co-seated together with Christ in heavenly places! We are identified in him. Col 3:1)*

3:15 We who have discovered our perfect righteousness have our thoughts anchored in Christ. If you still see yourself as imperfect, God will reveal to you that you are wasting your time to imagine that you can become more accepted and righteous than what you already are!

3:16 So then, let the message of grace set the pace. *(The law is a detour leading nowhere!)*

3:17 You are free to mimic me as we together impact the lives of many others to follow in our footsteps.

3:18 As you know I am often moved to tears talking about these things; I am so passionate about the revelation of mankind's redeemed innocence that it makes no sense to me that there can still be people who oppose this message. Many are openly hostile and indifferent to the cross of Christ.

3:19 Do they not realize that the DIY law-system leads to self-destruction? All their devotion to the god of their religious appetites, endorses their shame; yet they seem to have no problem with it since their minds are seared with [1]sin-consciousness. *("[1]Earthly things" in this case refers to the fallen mindset ruled by a sin-consciousness. See Col 3:1-3, Heb 10:1, 19-22)*

3:20 Our [1]citizenship is referenced in our joint position with Christ in heavenly places! Heaven is not our goal it is our [2]starting point! Our understanding is [3]sourced in a Savior; we [4]fully embrace the Lord Jesus Christ! *(The word, [1]politeuma, common wealth, our social identity. The word [2]uparcho, means to make a beginning, starting point. The word translated source is the word, [3]ek. To fully embrace, [4]apekdechomai, from apo, away from [that which defined me before] and ek, out of, source; and dechomai, to take into ones hands to accept whole heartedly, to fully embrace)*

3:21 The salvation that Jesus is the author of, refashions these bodies of clay and elevates us to fully participate in the same pattern of his heavenly glory! The severe contradiction that we might often face in the frailty of the flesh, is by far surpassed by the glorious splendor displayed in his human body raised from the dead; according to the working of God's dynamic power he imprints the mirror pattern of his likeness in us. Thus he subdues all things to himself. *(Paul's quest to fully comprehend the power of the resurrection (3:10) is consistent with his prayer in Eph 1:19 I pray that you will understand beyond all comparison the magnitude of his mighty power at work [1]in us who believe. Faith reveals how enormously advantaged we are in Christ. [The preposition [1]eis, speaks of a point reached in conclusion.] Eph 1:20 It is the same dynamic energy which God unleashed in Christ when he raised him from the dead and forever established him in the power of his own right hand in the realm of the heavens. Eph 1:21 Infinitely above all the combined forces of*

PHILIPPIANS Chaper 3

rule, authority, dominion, or governments; he is ranked superior to any name that could ever be given to anyone of this age or any age still to come in the eternal future. Eph 1:22 I want you to see this: he subjected all these powers under his feet. He towers head and shoulders above everything. He is the head; Eph 1:23 the [1]church is his body. The completeness of his being that fills all in all resides in us! God cannot make himself more visible or exhibit himself more accurately. [The word, [1]ekklesia, comes from ek, a preposition always denoting origin, and klesia from kaleo, to identify by name, to surname; thus the "church" is his redeemed image and likeness in mankind.]

See again Phil 2:6 His being God's equal in form and likeness was official; his sonship did not steal the limelight from his Father! Neither did his humanity distract from the deity of God! Phil 2:7 His mission however, was not to prove his deity but to embrace our humanity. He emptied himself into a physical human form; born in our resemblance he identified himself as the servant of the human race. His love enslaved him to us! Phil 2:8 And so we have the drama of the cross in context: the man Jesus Christ who is fully God, becomes fully man to the extent of willingly dying humanity's death at the hands of his own creation. He embraced the curse and shame of the lowest kind in dying a criminal's death. Phil 2:9 From this place of utter humiliation, God exalted him to the highest rank. God graced Jesus with a Name that is far [1]above as well as equally representative of every other name; [The word, [1]uper, means above, also instead, or for the sake of. The name of Jesus endorses his mission as fully accomplished! He is the Savior of the world! See also Eph 3:15, Every family in heaven and on earth originates in him; his is mankind's family name and he remains the authentic identity of every nation.] Phil 2:10 What his name unveils will persuade every creature of their redemption! Every knee in heaven and upon the earth and under the earth shall bow in spontaneous worship! Eph 4:8 Scripture confirms that he led us as trophies in his triumphant procession on high; he [1]repossessed his gift (likeness) in mankind. (See Ephesians 2:6, We are also elevated in his ascension to be equally welcome in the throne room of the heavenly realm where we are now seated together with him in his authority. Quote from the Hebrew text, Ps 68:18, [1]lakachta mattanoth baadam, thou hast taken gifts in human form, in Adam. [The gifts which Jesus Christ distributes to us he has received in us, in and by virtue of his incarnation. Commentary by Adam Clarke.] We were born anew in his resurrection. 1 Pet 1:3, Hos 6:2))

4:1 Now in the light of all this, I am sure that you can appreciate what enormous delight you are to me! My precious friends and brethern, you are my trophy and my joy! Just as you have been doing, continue to stand immovably strong in the Lord!

4:2 Your ¹source defines you by name! Dear ²Eodias and ³Syntyche, let me remind you of the meanings of your names! Engage your thoughts to follow the direct and easy way of grace; thus you will together fulfill your mission in the Lord without distraction. *(The word, ¹parakaleo, comes from para, a preposition indicating close proximity, a thing proceeding from a sphere of influence, with a suggestion of union of place of residence, to have sprung from its author and giver, originating from, denoting the point from which an action originates, intimate connection; and kaleo, meaning to identify by name, to surname. The word ²eudias, from eu, good, and odos, a road, thus a prosperous and expeditious journey, to lead by a direct and easy way; ³suntuche, from sun, together with, and tugchanō, to hit the mark; of one discharging a javelin or arrow)*

4:3 Suzegos, you are the meaning of your name to me; my trustworthy yoke fellow! Associate yourself closely with these ladies who have been my fellow athletes in the gospel! Also Clement as well as all my other colleagues I have their names on record in the book of life! *(Paul has all his friends names on record! [See Romans 16:1-23] Zoe life as defined in Christ has given such rich meaning to proper names. Suzugos, meaning yoke-fellow. At Philippi, women were the first hearers of the Gospel, and Lydia* *the first convert. Acts 16:13-15. **Clement**, clear skies, bright and sunny weather. Paul whose own name was changed from, **Sheol**, meaning dark underworld, to **Pao**, rest, appreciates the meaning of proper names. He calls Peter, Kefas which is the Aramaic for petros, to deliberately steer away from the more familiar sound of Petros, thus he specifically emphasizes the meaning of his name. The rock foundation of God's ekklesia. In Mat 16 Jesus identifies Simon, the son of Jonah by a new name, Petros; and upon this revelation, that the son of man is the son of God the ekklesia is built!)*

4:4 Joy is not a luxury option; joy is your constant! Your union in the Lord is your permanent source of delight; so I might as well say it again, rejoice in the Lord always!

4:5 Show perfect [1]courtesy towards all people! The Lord is not nearer to some than what he is to others! *(Courtesy, [1]**epieikes**, from **epi**, indicating continues influence upon, and **eikos**, reasonable, courteous. This is exactly Paul's attitude towards the idol worshipping Greek philosophers in Acts 17:27,28. See also Titus 3:3. Your joy makes the gospel visible! Every definition of distance is cancelled!)*

4:6 Let no anxiety about anything [1]distract you! Rather translate moments into prayerful worship, and soak your requests in gratitude before God! *(The word [1]**merimnao**, anxiety, through the idea of distraction, from **meritzo**, to divide. Your requests do not surprise God; he knows your thoughts from afar and is acquainted with all your ways; yet he delights in your con-*

versation and childlike trust! Song of Songs 2:14; Mat 6:8)

4:7 And in this place of worship and gratitude you will witness how the peace of God within you echoes the awareness of your oneness in Christ Jesus beyond the reach of any thought that could possibly unsettle you. *(uperecho)* **Just like the [1]sentry guard secures a city, watching out in advance for the first signs of any possible threat, your hearts deepest feelings and the tranquility of your thoughts are fully guarded there.** *(This peace is not measured by external circumstances, it is residing deeply in the innermost parts of your being. We are not talking about a fragile sense of peace that can easily be disturbed; one that we have to fabricate ourselves; this is God's peace; the peace that God himself enjoys!)*

4:8 Now let this be your conclusive [1]reasoning: consider that which is [2]true about everyone as evidenced in Christ. Live [3]overwhelmed by God's opinion of you! Acquaint yourselves with the revelation of [4]righteousness; realize God's likeness in you. Make it your business to declare mankind's redeemed [5]innocence. Think [6]friendship. Discover how [7]famous everyone is in the light of the gospel; mankind is in God's limelight! Ponder how [8]elevated you are in Christ. Study [9]stories that celebrate life. *(See Col 3:3, "Engage your thoughts with throne room realities where we are co-seated together with Christ!" The word [1]logitsomai suggests a logical reasoning by taking everything into account; [2]alethes, means that which was hidden, but is now uncovered; In Eph 3:21 Paul speaks about the*

PHILIPPIANS Chaper 4

truth as it is embodied in Jesus. The word overwhelmed is,
³semnos, from sebomai, to revere, to adore. The word for
righteousness is ⁴dikaios, from dikay, two parties finding
likeness in each other, where there is no sense of inferiority,
suspicion, blame, regret or pressure to perform. The gospel
is the revelation of the righteousness of God; it declares
how God succeeded to put mankind right with him. It is
about what God did right, not what Adam did wrong.
See Rom 1:17. The word ⁵hagnos speaks of blameless in-
nocence. The word ⁶prophileo, is exactly what it says,
pro-friendship. The English word for famous is derived
from the Greek word ⁷euphemos, from eu, well done, good
and phemos; it means to be in the lime light, from phao,
to shine; Jesus said, "you are the light of the world." Just
like a city set on a hill, your light cannot be hid. The word
⁸arete, is often translated, virtue, from airo, to raise up, to
elevate; ⁹epainos, commendable, praise worthy, from epi,
indicating continual influence upon, and ainos, story.)

**4:9 These things are consistent with all that I teach
and live; you can confidently practice what you hear
and see in me. The peace that inevitably follows
this lifestyle is more than a fuzzy feeling; this is
God himself endorsing our oneness.**

**4:10 I am so happy in the Lord that after all this time
you have shown such revived concern in my well-
being. It is refreshing to know your support, even
though you did not recently have the opportunity
to express it.**

**4:11 Hey, don't get me wrong, I am not hinting for
funding! I have discovered my "I am-ness" and**

found that I am fully ¹self sufficient, whatever the circumstance. *(Self sufficient, ¹autarkes, self complacent, the feeling you have when you are completely satisfied with yourself.)*

4:12 I am not defined by abuse or abundance! It might be a different day and a different place, but the secret remains the same; whether I am facing a feast or a fast, a fountain or famine. *(Abundance is not a sign of God's goodness; neither is lack a sign of his absence! "Righteousness by his (God's) faith defines life." The good news is the fact that the Cross of Christ was a success. God rescued the life of our design; he redeemed our innocence. Mankind would never again be judged righteous or unrighteous by their own ability to obey moral laws! It is not about what someone must or must not do but about what Jesus has done! It is from faith to faith, and not a person's good or bad behavior or circumstances interpreted as a blessing or a curse [Hab 2:4]. Instead of reading the curse when disaster strikes, Habakkuk realizes that the Promise out-dates performance as the basis to mankind's acquittal. Deuteronomy 28 would no longer be the motivation or the measure of right or wrong behavior! "Though the fig trees do not blossom, nor fruit be on the vines, the produce of the olive fail and the fields yield no food, the flock be cut off from the fold and there be no herd in the stalls, yet I will rejoice in the Lord, I will joy in the God of my salvation. God, the Lord, is my strength; he makes my feet like hinds' feet, he makes me tread upon my high places [Hab 3:17-19 RSV]. "Look away [from the law of works] unto Jesus; he is the Author and finisher of faith." [Heb 12:1]. See Rom 1:17.)*

PHILIPPIANS Chaper 4

4:13 In every situation I am strong in the one who empowers me from within to be who I am! *(Paul lived his life in touch with this place within himself. He discovered that the same I am-ness that Jesus walked in, was mirrored in him! I am what I am by the grace of God! Christ in me, mirrors Christ in you! Phil 2:12, "Not only in my presence but much more in my absence! Col 1:27 In us God desires to exhibit the priceless treasure of Christ's indwelling; every nation will recognize him as in a mirror! The unveiling of Christ in human life completes mankind's every expectation. He is not hiding in history, or in outer space nor in the future, neither in the pages of scripture, he is merely mirrored there to be unveiled within you. [Mt 13:44, Gal 1:15, 16.]*

4:14 Now I am not saying that I did not need or appreciate your help! Your joint participation in my difficult times was like beautiful poetry to me!

4:15 You and I know very well that your initial encounter with the gospel inspired you to partner with me in the wonderful rythm of giving and receiving. Your generosity then financed my trip in and out of Macedonia! No other church did what you did. *(Paul visited Thessalonica and Berea, about 12 years before this epistle was written. Acts 17: 1-14.)*

4:16 You also helped me several times in Thessalonica.

4:17 I am not reminding you of your gifts for any other reason but to encourage you to realize the abundant harvest in the word that you are a living epistle of. *(Greek, the fruit of "your word.")*

4:18 This letter is my official ¹receipt to you, proving that my capacity is filled to the brim! I am bursting at the seams indulging in your gifts that Epaphrodites brought! Your generosity celebrates God's pleasure like a sweet perfume poured out on the altar of your love for me. *(The word ¹apecho here is used as a commercial term meaning to receive a sum in full and give a receipt for it. From apo and echo, to hold; in this context the preposition apo with the accusative denotes correspondence of the contents to the capacity; of the possession to the desire. J.B. Lightfoot)*

4:19 My God shall also abundantly fill every nook and cranny to overflowing in all areas of your lives. The wealth of his dream come true in Christ Jesus measures his generosity towards you!

4:20 For countless ages upon ages God will be celebrated as our Father. We are his glory! Most certainly!

4:21 Embrace every saint in Christ Jesus on our behalf; the brethern with me embrace you!

4:22 All the saints, especially those within the household of Caesar greet you dearly!

4:23 The grace that Jesus Christ embodies embraces you in your spirit.

www.ingramcontent.com/pod-product-compliance
Lightning Source LLC
Chambersburg PA
CBHW070050070426
42449CB00012BA/3209